For

LOVE

Let Me Count the Ways

· · · · · · · · · · · ·

Viewing the Many
Faces of Love

By Dr. Rita Freedman

Design by Deborah Michel

PETER PAUPER PRESS, INC
WHITE PLAINS · NEW YORK

Copyright © 1994
Peter Pauper Press, Inc.
202 Mamaroneck Avenue
White Plains, NY 10601
ISBN 0-88088-878-4
Printed in Singapore
7 6 5 4 3 2 1

Jacket background painting by Linda DeVito Soltis
Jacket inset painting by Grace De Vito

Contents

LOVE
· · · · · · · · · · · ·
Let Me Count the Ways

$\mathcal{H}$ave you ever wondered how love between friends differs from love between mates? why first love seems so simple, marital love so complex? why certain relationships grow effortlessly while others need constant work? why women and men seem to approach love differently? why "love is blind but marriage is an eye-opener?"

$\mathcal{P}$erhaps it's because love, though fundamental to life, is such a distinctly personal experience. While everyone needs love, we don't all need it in the same way. And we each respond differently to the love that comes to us.

$\mathscr{I}$n addition, love isn't a static thing but a dynamic process that changes as we grow and mature. Right from birth, we respond naturally to touch, to smiles, and to tenderness. Being well loved, we are able to learn the art of loving. We learn to trust our own loving natures. The more we experience love that is gentle and loyal, the better we love back.

$\mathscr{S}$ome people seem to be born with a special knack for learning love's language; others must work hard to find their true loving voice. Read on, and discover your many voices of love. To paraphrase W. C. Fields, "some things are better than love, some things are worse, but there's nothing exactly like it."

$\mathscr{R}. \mathscr{F}.$

First
LOVE

Did you know?

When asked if they recall their first love, most people can easily come up with a full name and description.

Above all, first love is unforgettable.
Old diaries guard the secrets of those memorable firsts:
    first dance, first touch, first kiss.
From a tiny inner tingling to a pitter-patter fluttering,
    feelings gradually unfold into sweet infatuation.
The power of puppy love swings open the gates of
    childhood.
Will you ever forget that first dazzling glimpse of life's
    romantic possibilities?

How delicious is the winning
Of a kiss at love's beginning,
When two mutual hearts are sighing
For the knot there's no untying!

THOMAS CAMPBELL

Remember yesterday's date for it is a very important day
in my life. Surely it is an important day for any girl
when she receives her first kiss. . . . How it came about
so suddenly, I don't know, but before we went
downstairs, he kissed me. Through my hair, half on my
left cheek, half on my ear. I tore downstairs without
looking around, and am simply longing for tonight.

ANNE FRANK

I'm glad it cannot happen twice, the fever of first love.

DAPHNE DU MAURIER,
REBECCA

The first kiss is different from the thousandth, and the intensity of the passionate feeling of young or new love is different in some way from romantic love that has matured in time.

WILLARD GAYLIN

The first love is only a little foolishness and a lot of curiosity: no really self-respecting woman would take advantage of it.

GEORGE BERNARD SHAW

We learn how to love only when we are loved.

WILLIAM MENNINGER

Love and eggs are best when they are fresh.

RUSSIAN PROVERB

Feminine
LOVE

Did you know?

Women feel the ecstasy and the agony of romantic love more intensely than men and are willing to discuss their feelings more openly.

For women, love of self and love of others feel
    inseparable.
Daughters are trained to stay closely connected; good
    girls don't roam too far from home.
As the guardians of family life, females nurture love
    with cards and calls and celebrations.
Reaching out with words to keep in touch, they build
    lasting connections, and find their collection of
    loved ones grows ever larger.

Yes, it's important to treat others as we ourselves would wish to be treated. But for women, the challenge is to treat ourselves as well as we treat others. After all, who wants a Golden Rule administered by a masochist?

GLORIA STEINEM

♥

Men always want to be a woman's first love—women like to be a man's last romance.

OSCAR WILDE

♥

What I expect from my male friends is that they are polite and clean. What I expect from my female friends is unconditional love, the ability to finish my sentences for me when I am sobbing, a complete and total willingness to pour their hearts out to me, and the ability to tell me why the meat thermometer isn't supposed to touch the bone.

ANNA QUINDLEN

Masculine
LOVE

Did you know?

Men have fewer close relationships in
their lives and less frequent contact with
the loved ones whom they do value.

The bonds of masculine love are somewhat fragile.
We train our sons toward independence, applaud them
*   as they separate to stand apart and on their own.*
Manly love is often action oriented.
Boys connect by tossing balls, tackling teammates,
*   talking sports.*
Power and competition are part of masculine intimacy,
*   and love becomes a game of winning, losing, and*
*   keeping score.*

Only when a man feels a strong, supportive link with other men . . . will he feel safe from his fears of engulfment in the feminine side of life. . . . If he is to be a truly nurturing man, he badly needs to have felt nurtured by men.

AUGUSTUS Y. NAPIER

♥

In love women are professionals, men are amateurs.

FRANÇOIS TRUFFAUT

♥

A man falls in love through his eyes. A woman through her ears.

WOODROW WYATT

♥

Love is the whole history of a woman's life; it is but an episode in a man's.

MADAME DE STAËL

Romantic
LOVE

Did you know?

Our culture assumes that sooner or later everyone will fall in love romantically. Perhaps that's why over 90% of college students say they have already fallen, at least once.

Mention love and romance springs to mind.
Romantic lovers are charmed by the best that each has
    to offer.
It's not the person so much as the act of loving that
    makes the beloved so enchanting.
While romantic love always fades with time and
    familiarity, it may evolve, before it dies, into deep
    and enduring love everlasting.

Being in love is better than being in jail, a dentist's chair, or a holding pattern over Philadelphia, but not if he doesn't love you back.

JUDITH VIORST

♥

I believe myself that romantic love is the source of the most intense delights that life has to offer. In the relation of a man and a woman who love each other with passion and imagination and tenderness, there is something of inestimable value, to be ignorant of which is a great misfortune to any human being.

BERTRAND RUSSELL

♥

In real love you want the other person's good. In romantic love you want the other person.

MARGARET ANDERSON

The history of a love affair is the drama of its fight against time.

PAUL GERALDY

One of the nicest things about it [love] is that it seems to splash over into all other areas of life, making the person in love a little more patient, more forgiving, and just a nicer human being in general.

LINDA L. ELROD

In every love affair, there is one who loves and one who permits himself to be loved.

W. WALLER

The type of human being we prefer reveals the contours of our heart.

ORTEGA Y GASSET

In a great romance, each person basically plays a part that the other really likes.

ELIZABETH ASHLEY

Courtly
LOVE

Did you know?

Valentine's Day originated in a pagan love festival that took place in mid-February on the feast day of St. Valentine, the patron saint of lovers.

Every day is Valentine's Day for courtly lovers.
Armed with chocolate and roses, they take up Cupid's
*   hunt for the pure pleasure of pursuit.*
They strut, they preen, they flash their fancy feathers.
In the game of courtly love, wooing is as much fun as
*   winning.*

When a man loves with all his heart there is a stirring within his soul. At times it is a feeling approaching worship for the woman. At other times he is fascinated, enchanted and amused. . . . There is a tenderness, an overwhelming desire to protect and shelter his woman from all harm, danger and difficulty of life.

H. B. ANDELIN

♥

To be in love is merely to be in a state of perceptual anesthesia—to mistake an ordinary young man for a Greek god or an ordinary young woman for a goddess.

H. L. MENCKEN

♥

Love is an attempt to change a piece of a dream-world into reality.

THEODORE REIK

Passionate LOVE

Did you know?

Men fall into passionate love very fast, whereas females are more cautious about letting passion take them over.

Beware! Eros packs a powerful punch.
Passionate love excites the mind, delights the eye, ignites
  a spark that sets your heart on fire.
Take care: The joys of lusty love are bewitching.
Cast under its spell, you'll stumble out of control, drunk
  with desire, and full of your own desirability.

Ecstasy cannot last, but it can carve a channel for something lasting.

E. M. FORSTER

♥

Love is the strange bewilderment which overtakes one person on account of another person.

JAMES THURBER AND E. B. WHITE

♥

A kiss is a lovely trick designed by nature to stop speech when words become superfluous.

INGRID BERGMAN

♥

…and then I asked him with my eyes to ask again yes…
and first I put my arms around him yes…
and his heart was going like mad
and yes I said yes I will Yes.

JAMES JOYCE,
ULYSSES

Jealous LOVE

Did you know?

A great many societies permit men to have several wives, but women are almost never permitted more than one husband.

How sweet to be loved exclusively—adored as the one
  and only. Jealousy takes root when someone divides
  a bonded pair.
When a new baby shifts a Mom's love from her
  firstborn.
When a neighbor shifts a man's eye from his wife.
The more secure you are in a relationship, the less
  jealousy will disrupt that love.

No matter how perfect—or practically perfect—a wife may be, she always has to watch out for the Other Woman. The Other Woman, according to my definition, is anyone able to charm my husband, amuse my husband, attract my husband, or occupy his wholehearted interest for more than 30 seconds straight.

JUDITH VIORST

♥

    O! beware, my lord, of jealousy;
It is the green-eyed monster which
  doth mock
The meat it feeds on . . .

WILLIAM SHAKESPEARE,
OTHELLO

♥

Set me as a seal upon thine heart, as a seal upon thine arm: for love is strong as death; jealousy is cruel as the grave.

SOLOMON'S SONG 8:6 (KJV)

Marital
LOVE

Did you know?

Married people list the following characteristics as most important in a mate: consideration, honesty, affection, intelligence, kindness, understanding, loyalty, and being an interesting companion.

If love is blind, then marriage is an eye opener.
Marriage vows weave couples into complex family
systems.
Love between spouses isn't static but dynamic.
It cycles over time, waxing and waning as mates evolve.
For some lucky couples, this loving process really does
last a lifetime.

In the opinion of the world, marriage ends all, as it does in a comedy. The truth is precisely the opposite: it begins all.

ANNE SOPHIE SWETCHINE

An archeologist is the best husband any woman can have: the older she gets, the more interested he is in her.

AGATHA CHRISTIE

Where there's marriage without love, there will be love without marriage.

BEN FRANKLIN

A life *allied* with mine, for the rest of our lives—that is the miracle of marriage.

DENIS DE ROUGEMONT

Falling in love is a trick that our genes pull on our otherwise perceptive mind to hoodwink or trap us into marriage.

M. SCOTT PECK

♥

One advantage of marriage, it seems to me, is that when you fall out of love with him, or he falls out of love with you, it keeps you together until you maybe fall in again.

JUDITH VIORST

♥

My husband's the only man I ever met whom I feel totally emotionally supported by without competing or feeling scared. I can be who I am because he is my rock . . . He gives me something I never had, even with my father—a safe harbor. And nothing in marriage is more important than that.

VICTORIA SECUNDA,
QUOTING HELENE, THIRTY-SEVEN, IN A CASE STUDY

Two people holding each other up like flying buttresses. Two people depending on each other and babying each other and defending each other against the world outside. Sometimes it was worth all the disadvantages of marriage just to have that: one friend in an indifferent world.

ERICA JONG

Marriage is the antidote to romance.

OLD SAYING

Love is the free exercise of choice. Two people love each other only when they are quite capable of living without each other but *choose* to live with each other.

M. SCOTT PECK

Lost LOVE

Did you know?

Because many divorced women never remarry, and because wives tend to outlive their husbands, two out of three women over 65 are unmarried.

Loss of love is one of the hazards of having it.
Though parting is sweet sorrow, still it is "better to have
    loved and lost than never to have loved at all."
We grow out of love, or simply outgrow it.
Paths diverge.
Dear ones move on to new fields, leaving us behind.
Yet out of the pain of lost love sprout new possibilities.

Had we never loved so kindly,
Had we never loved so blindly,
Never met or never parted,
We had ne'er been broken-hearted.

ROBERT BURNS

♥

. . . I love thee with the breath,
Smiles, tears, of all my life!—and, if God choose,
I shall but love thee better after death.

ELIZABETH BARRETT BROWNING

♥

To love means to embrace and at the same time to
withstand many many endings, and many many
beginnings—all in the same relationship.

CLARISSA PINKOLA ESTÉS

Friendly LOVE

Did you know?

While male friends typically enjoy *doing* things together, female friends seem content just *being* together.

Companions come in a rainbow of colors.
Workmates, playmates, soulmates offer countless forms
of love.
Our friends are our chosen family, and the bonds of
friendship can be as strong as those of blood or
marriage. Best friends may love us just as much
and know us even better than our Moms or our mates.

What I cannot love, I overlook. Is that real friendship?

ANAÏS NIN

Love is a friendship that has caught fire. It is quiet understanding, mutual confidence, sharing and forgiving. It is a loyalty through good and bad. It settles for less than perfection and makes allowances for human weaknesses.

ANN LANDERS

We cannot tell the precise moment when friendship is formed. As in filling a vessel drop by drop, there is at last a drop which makes it run over; so in a series of kindnesses there is at last one which makes the heart run over.

JAMES BOSWELL

Body
LOVE

Did you know?

People who love their own bodies have higher self-esteem and greater intimacy in their lives than those who suffer from poor body image.

Like the mythical Narcissus, you can fall in love with your own image simply by seeing it through more loving eyes.

If you behold your body as you would a beloved, if you tune into its gentle messages and treat it as tenderly as you would a dear friend, it will teach you a lot about loving and being loved. You'll discover through body love a healing harmony between mind and body.

We all have the potential to love our bodies. Like any loving relationship it takes work to realize that potential.

RITA FREEDMAN

♥

Why not fall in love with the body you've been sleeping with all your life?

STEWART EMERY

♥

Here's my morning ritual. I open a sleepy eye, take one horrified look at my reflection in the mirror and then repeat with conviction: "I'm me and I'm wonderful. Because God doesn't make junk."

ERMA BOMBECK

♥

As you learn to fill up your senses with lovely feelings and become a more sensuous woman, you'll start to look lovelier in your own eyes.

RITA FREEDMAN

Self
LOVE

Did you know?

Self love influences your judgments of how others feel about you. People with high self-esteem are tuned in to hearing praise, while those with low self-esteem are always listening for criticism.

Every self is lovable, including you.
Can you honor yourself with the gift of love?
Perfection isn't necessary.
You're worthy of self love just as you are.
By embracing your flaws, your faults, your childish
*   fears, you'll find acceptance of the flaws in others.*

Being loved anyway is not being regarded as perfect but being accepted as imperfect.

ELLEN GOODMAN

♥

As I love myself, it is only a short step to the loving of others.

ANNE WILSON SCHAEF

♥

The image of myself which I try to create in my own mind that I may love myself is very different from the image which I try to create in the minds of others in order that they may love me.

W. H. AUDEN

♥

"Love thy neighbor as thyself" assumes that you *do* love yourself. Note that it does not say *"instead of* thyself" but *"as* thyself."

L. MADOW

Love is the increase of self by means of others.

SPINOZA

There are many more people trying to *meet* the right person than to become the right person.

GLORIA STEINEM

Love is the only thing you get more of by giving it away.

TOM WILSON

The love we give away is the only love we keep.

ELBERT HUBBARD

In profound love, it *is* as blessed to give as to receive. Such love is not unselfish love, of course. We give to ourselves when we give to the other.

E. WALSTER AND G. W. WALSTER

You need someone to love you while you're looking for someone to love.

SHELAGH DELANEY

Family LOVE

Did you know?

We tend to reconstruct the same kinds of love relationships in our adult families that we learned in our families of birth.

Life feels safer when you can come home to family love.
Family boundaries keep changing to make room for
  relatives long lost or just found, for in-laws and step-
  folks and great aunts inherited, adopted, or chosen as
  family.
When extended far enough, all our family trees would
  overlap, forming a universal human family.
Imagine the power of family love, flowing freely across those
  branches.

To love our children is to see them, respect them, share life with them . . . and always to let go.

ANNE WILSON SCHAEF

It is within the families themselves where peace can begin. If families can learn to respect their members, and deal with conflict resolution, that would be the first step to keeping peace on a global level.

SUSAN PARTNOW

The family is one of nature's masterpieces.

GEORGE SANTAYANA

If you cannot get rid of the family skeleton, you may as well make it dance.

GEORGE BERNARD SHAW

Filial
LOVE

Did you know?

When college students were asked to name a person they highly respected, they overwhelmingly chose one of their parents.

Filial love is learned in small lessons across a lifetime.
Parents' arms are there, outstretched to cheer us when
*   we win and catch us when we fail.*
Who will give back love to parents as they age?
Children who know that most mothers and fathers have
*   simply tried to do their best.*

My mother . . . is a much-loved, much-admired
grandmother . . . she lives in the present and future,
not the past. . . . In writing these pages, I am admitting,
at least, how important her existence is and has been
for me.

ADRIENNE RICH

How are we to be the mothers we want our daughters to
have, if we are still sorting out who our own mothers are
and what they mean to us?

LETTY COTTIN POGREBIN

My mother . . . has taught me many lessons:
Nothing is as it appears.
There are no calories in a broken cookie.
When in doubt, throw it out. . . .
Never trust anyone with a secret—except your mother.

IRENE ZAHAVA

Motherly LOVE

Did you know?

When newborn chimps are deprived of mother love they grow up to be anxious adults who can't get along with others or take proper care of their own babies.

Mother love is like no other love.
Essential and primary, it builds basic trust in all future
  relationships.
A mother's touch awakens joy in human contact.
A mother's praise echoes across a lifetime.
Mothers are supposed to love us unconditionally, just
  because we exist.
Miraculously, some Moms are able to do just that.

My mother had a great deal of trouble with me, but I think she enjoyed it.

MARK TWAIN

♥

Many of us were mothered in ways we cannot yet even perceive; we only know that our mothers were in some incalculable way on our side.

ADRIENNE RICH

♥

The mother's heart is the child's schoolroom.

HENRY WARD BEECHER

♥

I have heard daughters say that they do not love their mothers. I have *never* heard a mother say she does not love her daughter.

NANCY FRIDAY

Fatherly
LOVE

Did you know?

Fathers' involvement with their children is greatest in monogamous cultures, where men's work allows easy access to their children, and where women's work outside the home is valued.

Here's to all the men now striving to become the loving
*   Dad they always wished they had.*
Father love is a precious thing.
Most of us long for more of it.
We long for strong Dads, who are there with support.
And for smart Dads, who will teach us about life.

My kids assume that there is nothing Dad cannot do. They think I know everything . . . They think I'm a hero, and they don't know that I'm really not. Why don't they know? Maybe because I'm afraid to tell them.

VICTORIA SECUNDA,
QUOTING MICHAEL, SIXTY-ONE, IN A CASE STUDY

♥

When I was in fifth grade and big and fat and taller than the other kids, he would tell me I was his "long-stemmed rose." To this day, I stand straight, with pride, and try to think of myself as my father's long-stemmed rose.

ANONYMOUS

♥

The most important thing a father can do for his children is to love their mother.

THEODORE MARTIN HESBURGH

Brotherly
LOVE

Did you know?

Eldest brothers use their greater power to support,
protect and also control younger siblings. Their position
as the family leader continues into old age.

Brotherly love—a universal ideal to unite the global
family in a fraternal embrace. Men band in
brotherhood to loyally defend a country or a cause.
Compared to their sisters, brothers talk less and compete
more.
Remembrances of all the games won and fights lost in the
course of brotherly love leave lasting imprints on
human fellowship.

Brotherhood is not so wild a dream as those who profit by postponing it pretend.

ERIC SEVAREID

If we are not our brother's keeper, let us at least not be his executioner.

MARLON BRANDO

It's becoming clear to us that manhood doesn't happen by itself; it doesn't happen just because we eat Wheaties. The active intervention of the older men means that older men welcome the younger man into the ancient, mythologized, instinctive male world.

ROBERT BLY

Sisterly LOVE

Did you know?

The relationship between sisters is typically more intimate and more intense than between any other sibling combination.

In sisterhood there is tender power.
Older sisters serve as family caretakers.
Younger ones enjoy the role of pampered princess.
As jealous rivals, sisters battle over beauty and boyfriends.
Yet closely identified, the fabric of their love is tightly woven.
Sharing clothes and makeup, secrets and truth, women
     become true sisters under the skin.

Sisters is probably *the* most competitive relationship within the family, but once the sisters are grown, it becomes the strongest relationship.

MARGARET MEAD

♥

You know full as well as I do the value of sisters' affections to each other; there is nothing like it in this world.

CHARLOTTE BRONTË

♥

Dear Santa: My turtle died. I hope my sister's turtle dies too.

ANONYMOUS,
QUOTED BY FRANCINE KLAGSBRUN

♥

Never praise a sister to a sister, in the hope of your compliments reaching the proper ears.

RUDYARD KIPLING

Grandparental
LOVE

Did you know?

As life expectancy increases, over half the children born today have four living grandparents, many of whom will live to see their grandchildren grow to adulthood.

The very old and the very young need each other for that
special grand love which flows across generations.
Lucky the child with a doting Grandma who has lots of free
time for teaching and touching.
Lucky the Grandpa whose life is enriched by the curious
questions and glorious hugs of his child's child.

Being a grandparent is one of the best things that can happen to you. The only trouble is you have to be a parent first.

ADELE FREEDMAN

♥

We are able to accept, even love, things in our grandparents that we find impossible to accept in their children, our parents. The reverse is true, too: in us they can take the joys without the responsibilities.

ANNA QUINDLEN

♥

What impressed me about my grandmother was not only her beauty, but her perfume, cigarettes, coffee, cardplaying, jewelry and incessant social life, all of which caused her to be considered a *bad* mother in the family . . . I loved her more than I've loved anyone.

LOUISE BERNIKOW

Seasoned
LOVE

Did you know?

Love is more likely to last if both partners feel they are
making a fairly equal contribution to the relationship,
and getting an equal return.

Seasoned love is like a rich stew that has simmered until its
full flavor bubbles up.
Basic ingredients are commitment and flexibility, with taste
enhanced by sweet memories, salty tears, and mellow
moments added slowly over time.
When stirred with daily affection, its delicate aroma drifts
into the future.
Enduring love can nourish and sustain you with hearty
satisfaction.

Immature love says: "I love you because I need you."
Mature love says: "I need you because I love you."

ERICH FROMM

The memories of long love gather like drifting snow,
poignant as the mandarin ducks who float side by side
in sleep.

LADY MURASAKI

However old a conjugal union, it still garners some
sweetness. Winter has some cloudless days, and under
the snow a few flowers still bloom.

MADAME DE STAËL

Spiritual
LOVE

Did you know?

The marital vows of most religions create a sacred bond by interweaving a couple's love with that of a higher spiritual power.

Spiritual love can unlock the mysteries of every other kind of love.

Have you ever prayed for love, and in the silence of your self-reflection discovered that love was already yours?

A spiritual awakening breathes life into a sleeping soul.

If God is love, then love is also divine.

To love deeply is to fulfill one's holy potential.

Love is a flame which burns in heaven, and whose soft reflections radiate to us. Two worlds are opened, two lives given to it. It is by love that we double our being; it is by love that we approach God.

AIMEE MARTIN

♥

And when Love speaks, the voice of all the gods
Makes heaven drowsy with the harmony.

WILLIAM SHAKESPEARE

♥

I never knew how to worship until I knew how to love.

HENRY WARD BEECHER

♥

The main reason for healing is love.

PARACELSUS

The universe is but one great city, full of beloved ones, divine and human by nature, endeared to each other.

EPICTETUS

♥

For one human being to love another: that is perhaps the most difficult of all our tasks, the ultimate, the last test and proof, the work for which all other work is but preparation.

RAINER MARIA RILKE

♥

Next to the love between man and his Creator . . . the love of one man and one woman is the loftiest and the most illusive ideal that has been set before the world. A perfect marriage is like a pure heart: those who have it are fit to see God.

ELIZABETH STUART PHELPS